This is Daniel Cook
at the Farm

Kids Can Press

This is Daniel Cook.
He likes to go different places,
meet interesting people and
try new things.

Mostly I like to have fun!

Today Daniel is visiting a farm.

Here we are!

This is Laura. She's going
to show Daniel around.

There are many different kinds of farms.
Some farmers grow crops, such as wheat
or vegetables. Other farmers raise animals,
such as sheep or chickens.

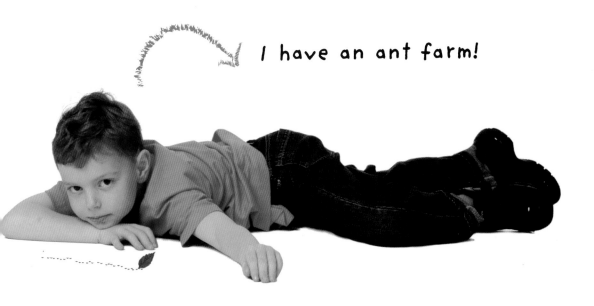

I have an ant farm!

The farm Daniel is visiting is small and has a
few different animals. Let's go meet them!

This is Susie. She's a ewe, a female sheep. Ewes give birth to one or two lambs every spring. Male sheep are called rams.

Springtime is also shearing time, when the sheep's soft fleece is clipped, or shorn, to make wool.

The fleece has to be shorn in one piece, like a coat. It takes a skilled shearer to do this — a very strong one, too! The shearer has to hold the sheep still while clipping the fleece. One sheep can produce up to 6 kg (13 lbs.) of wool a year.

Whoa! That's more than my head weighs!

Both sheep and goats eat grass and hay to stay healthy. A female goat is called a doe. A male goat is a buck. These are baby goats. They're called kids.

Some goats are raised for their fur just like sheep. They're shorn twice a year and produce mohair, a fuzzy kind of wool. Other goats are milked just like cows. You can drink goat's milk or use it to make cheese.

Hey! I'm a kid!

Cows on dairy farms are milked once or twice a day. Today cows are milked by machines, but long ago, cows were milked by hand. This is Kathryn. She's going to show Daniel how to milk a cow.

First I cleaned the cow's udder with a wet sponge.

Then I squeezed one of the teats — just a bit — and the milk squirted right into the bucket!

After Kathryn strained the milk, she let me taste it. It was good, but I think I like chocolate milk better!

Like cows and other animals, chickens eat feed. Feed is a mix of oats and corn or wheat and other grains, kind of like the cereal you eat. Chickens also like roasted soybeans and bugs and worms they can peck at in the dirt.

Worms? Yuck! I like strawberries in my cereal.

A female chicken is called a hen.
A male is called a rooster. Hens lay
about 300 eggs a year — that's almost one
egg every day! Some eggs are taken to eat.
Others are left to hatch. A hen will sit on
her eggs, turning them several times a day,
until they hatch 21 days later.

Baby chicks begin to grow their feathers
two or three days after they hatch.

A mother pig, or sow, carries her babies for 115 days.

That's a lot of brothers and sisters!

She gives birth to litters of 6 to 12 piglets. The piglets drink their mother's milk for about 28 days.

Have you ever seen a pig roll in the mud? Pigs are clean animals, but if it gets too hot, they cover themselves in mud to cool down. The mud also protects them from insect bites and sunburn.

Farmers often use pig poop, or manure, to fertilize their fields. It helps the crops grow.

This donkey's name is Dusty.

On the farm, donkeys pull carts or carry loads on their backs. Sometimes donkeys also help to protect sheep.
If a donkey grows up with a group, or flock, of sheep, it will think of them as family and keep them safe from other animals like wolves.

On cattle farms, horses are used to move the animals from one part of the pasture to the other for feeding or to round them up and drive them to shelter. Horse-riding farmers are sometimes called cowboys, cowgirls or cowpokes!

Yee-haw!

Before there were tractors, horses were used to plow and clear fields and pull wagons during the harvest on crop farms.

Helper animals on farms aren't always as big as donkeys or horses. Cats and dogs are good company for farmers and have important jobs on the farm, too. Cats help to keep mice and rats out of the barn and away from the feed. They also chase them out of the house!

Dogs guard the house and stand watch. They warn the farmer of foxes or weasels or hawks near the chicken coop. And they help round up, or herd, the sheep and cows, too, and keep them safe from other animals like wolves or snakes or coyotes.

I met all kinds of animals at the farm. Now it's your turn to play — on a finger-puppet farm!

You will need
- felt
- white craft glue or fabric glue
- small googly eyes
- a fabric marker
- pipe cleaners (optional)
- a pencil, a ruler, safety scissors

1. For the body, cut out two 4 cm x 6 cm (1 1/2 in. x 2 1/2 in.) pieces of felt.

2. Squeeze a skinny line of glue onto three edges of one felt piece. Then place the other piece on top and gently press the pieces together. Put aside.

3. For the head, cut out a felt circle 4 cm (1¹/₂ in.) in diameter.

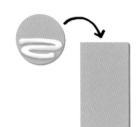

4. Glue the bottom half of the head onto the body.

5. Glue the googly eyes onto the face.

6. If you're making a pig, dog, cow or goat, cut out ear shapes and glue them on.

7. For a nose or a mouth, either cut out shapes and glue them on, or draw them on. Now add fun details, like spots for a cow or a curly pipe cleaner tail for a pig!

Based on the TV series *This is Daniel Cook*. Concept created by J.J. Johnson and Blair Powers. Produced by marblemedia and Sinking Ship Productions Inc.

Kids Can Press acknowledges the financial support of the Government of Ontario, through the Ontario Media Development Corporation's Ontario Book Initiative; the Ontario Arts Council; the Canada Council for the Arts; and the Government of Canada, through the BPIDP, for our publishing activity.

The producers of *This is Daniel Cook* acknowledge the support of Treehouse TV, TVOntario, other broadcast and funding partners and the talented, hard-working crew that made *This is Daniel Cook* a reality. In addition, they acknowledge the support and efforts of Deb, Murray and the Cook family, as well as Karen Boersma, Sheila Barry and Valerie Hussey at Kids Can Press.

Published in Canada by
Kids Can Press Ltd.
29 Birch Avenue
Toronto, ON M4V 1E2

Published in the U.S. by
Kids Can Press Ltd.
2250 Military Road
Tonawanda, NY 14150

www.kidscanpress.com

Written by Yvette Ghione
Edited by Karen Li
Illustrations and design by Céleste Gagnon
With special thanks to Laura Gow and Kathryn Cruickshank of Riverdale Farm

Printed and bound in China

The hardcover edition of this book is smyth sewn casebound.
The paperback edition of this book is limp sewn with a drawn-on cover.

Kids Can Press is a LORUS™ Entertainment company

CM 06 0 9 8 7 6 5 4 3 2 1
CM PA 06 0 9 8 7 6 5 4 3 2 1

Visit Daniel online at **www.thisisdanielcook.com**

Library and Archives Canada Cataloguing in Publication

Ghione, Yvette

    This is Daniel Cook at the farm / written by Yvette Ghio

ISBN-13: 978-1-55453-077-9 (bound)
ISBN-10: 1-55453-077-6 (bound)
ISBN-13: 978-1-55453-078-6 (pbk.)
ISBN-10: 1-55453-078-4 (pbk.)

1. Farms—Juvenile literature. 2. Domestic animals—Juveni
literature. 3. Farm life—Juvenile literature. I. Title.

SF75.5.G49 2006   j636   C2006-900740-

Photo Credits

Every reasonable effort has been made to trace ownership of, and give accurate credit to, copyrighted material. Information that would enable the publisher to correct any discrepancies in future editions would be appreciated.

cover: (goat) © iStockphoto.com/Redbull_UK; p. 7: (sheep) © iStockphoto.com/smilingworld; p. 15: (pigs) Royalty-free/C p. 21: (dog with sheep) Kevin R. Morris/Corbis; p. 23: (finger puppets) Frank Baldassarra; THIS IS DANIEL COOK gallery ph by Cylla Von Tiedemann; THIS IS DANIEL COOK location pho by Peter Stranks; all remaining photos © 2006 Jupiterimages Corporation.